THE ṚG VEDA AS LAND NAMA BOK

THE ṚG VEDA AS LAND NAMA BOK

By

ANANDA K. COOMARASWAMY

GYAN

Published by

Gyan Publishing House
5, Ansari Road
Daryaganj, New Delhi-110002
Phone: 011-47034999, 9811692060
E-mail: books@gyanbooks.com

Distribution Network
gyanbooks.com
India, USA, Canada, UK, Australia, France

ISBN : 978-81-212-2690-5 (HB)
First Published, 1935

2nd Impression 2021

Printed at: Gyan Press, Delhi.

The RG Veda AS Land Nama Bok
Author: Ananda K. Coomaraswamy

THE RG VEDA AS LAND-NÁMA-BÓK

By

ANANDA K. COOMARASWAMY

LONDON
LUZAC & CO.
46 GREAT RUSSELL STREET, W.C.1.
1935

DEDICATED TO

WALTER ANDRAE

AUTHOR OF

Die ionische Säule, Bauform oder Symbol?

AND TO

CARL ANDERS SCHARBAU

AUTHOR OF

Die Idee der Schöpfung in der vedischen Literatur

FIG. 1. Śrī Sūryôdaya, the "Holy Sunrise." From a sixteenth century MS. of the *Kalpa Sūtra* Museum of Fine Arts, Boston, see Brown, *Miniature paintings of the Jaina Kalpasūtra*, 1934, fig. 38.

The Dawn depicted is that of the day following Triśalā's announcement of her pregnancy dreams to Siddhârtha and is therefore that of the day of Mahāvīra's conception. Mahāvīra being, no less than the Buddha, the Solar Messiah, the Sunrise on the morning of his conception is virtually and, if we ignore the pseudo-historical presentation of the "miraculous" elements in the Jina's life, is actually the Coming Forth of the Hidden Light in the Beginning.

The designation Śrī Sūryôdaya appears as a legend in Nāgarī characters beside the illustration on the manuscript page. The text, § 59, describes the rising of the Sun as follows: "Early in the wane of night the Sun arose . . . intensely red. . . . He, the thousand-rayed Day-maker, glowing in fiery-energy, awakened the clusters of lotuses . . . by the blows of his hands the darkness was dispelled."

INTRODUCTION

In the Ṛg Veda, the Five Aryan kindreds are spoken of as immigrants; they have come from another place across the waters, and have settled and tilled the lands on the hither shore. This process of land-taking has generally been interpreted as referring to an historical immigration of an Aryan speaking people who, fair in colour and sharply distinguished from the dusky pagan Dasyus, crossed the Sarasvatī in the Panjab and made their home in Bharatavarṣa. That is an euhemeristic interpretation of a traditional literature which is strictly speaking devoid of any historical content whatever. We do not mean to say by this that there may not have taken place historical events analogous to those alluded to in the Vedic "myths"; on the contrary, we assume that history is always enacted in the pattern of the ultimate reality enunciated in the metaphysical tradition, or in Biblical phraseology, "that it might be fulfilled which was spoken by the prophets" (*ṛṣayaḥ*). It may therefore be true that the metaphysical tradition itself can by a process of inversion be employed by the historian as source material, just as an icon may be used by the æsthete as a piece of bric-a-brac, or by the anthropologist for his own ends. In this sense, for example, we may be sure that the people who performed the Vedic ritual and chanted the *mantras* in their recorded form, actually possessed horses and chariots, had experience of the crossing of seas and rivers, and tilled the soil. It does not follow that the cosmic myth itself—"originale Geistesschöpfung allerersten Ranges"[1]—had been unknown previous to that late stage of neolithic culture that is reflected in the symbolism of the *mantras* in which it is expressed. Certain of the symbols are by no means "dated"; the Sun may have been referred to as a bird at any time, nor can it be doubted that a cult of the One Madonna existed already in the Paleolithic age. The symbols that imply a specific cultural niveau may, simultaneously with actual invention, have been developed from earlier prototypes; before the pillar, the tree; before the wheel, the swastika; before the plough, the planting-stick.[2] It is in this sense that the myth itself, apart from the manner of its formulation (and this will apply even to its late recension in the two great pseudo-historical epics), may not be properly regarded as an historical relation (*itihāsa*), nor as concerned with events in time, but as a metaphysical formulation in accordance with a logical order of thought. Other versions of the "single and unanimous tradition," Genesis for example, are to be understood and have been understood in the same way. In like manner, the miraculous elements in the lives of the Messiahs are not to be regarded as later accretions imposed upon an historical nucleus, but much rather as parts of the essential theme to which an aspect of historicity has been superadded by way of accommodation (*upāya*).

To some students, these will seem to be self-evident theses, needing no demonstration. To others, merely a fantastic theory. With the latter in view it is proposed to discuss the matter in greater detail, by an analysis of the meanings and content of certain constantly recurring and characteristic terms, viz., *ārya*, *carṣaṇi* and *kṛṣṭi*, *pañca jana*, *sarasvatī*, *setu*, *vāpa-maṅgala*, *viśa* and *viśpati*, *yajña*, and *Yama*. If the proper interpretation of some of these terms is still a matter of controversy, it may nevertheless appear that some further light can be shed on the problems by a choice of valid interpretations of such sort that all the terms can be understood consistently in relation to one another or in one and the same context.[3]

THE ṚG VEDA AS LAND-NÁMA-BÓK

ĀRYA, ARYA

Ārya, " noble " or " gentle " (as in " gentleman ") is from *ṛ*, to go, rise up, reach, obtain ; cognate forms are *ariya*, *airya*, Irān, Erin, and Germ. Ehre ; for the root, cf. Zend *ir*, Lith *ir-ti* (to row, cf. Skr. *aritra*, " oar "), Greek *'ór-nu-mi*, *'aró-o*, etc., and Lat. *or-ior*, *or-iens*. Any connection with Lat. *ar*, to plough, may be doubted. The root meanings give the sense of going forward and taking possession. The root meaning of *ārya* is that of " pioneer," in the American sense, where the first settlers are most highly honoured (one might almost speak of an " ancestral cult " in this connection), and where it represents the height of social distinction to be descended from these first-comers from the other side. From this point of view there develops the secondary meaning of " noble " and that of " right," cf. *ṛta* " law " and *ari* " loyal " ; the procedure of the first settlers being thought of as an establishment of law and order where savagery (*anṛta*) had previously prevailed.[4] Thus he, Agni, who *pūrvam ārta* (RV., IV, 1, 12) is not only *ṛtajā* and *ṛtâyus*, but also *ṛtavān* and *ṛtvij*, or in short and in every sense of the word, *ārya* or *arya*.[5]

It need hardly be pointed out that the term *ārya* is applied by the Aryans themselves to themselves in this laudatory sense, and by way of distinction from others whose descent and behaviour are relatively abominated, and of whose point of view we hear little.[6]

THE ṚG VEDA AS LAND-NÁMA-BÓK

CARṢAṆI AND KṚṢṬI

Carṣaṇi and *kṛṣṭi*, "ploughman" and "ploughing," or "tilling" and "tilth," are both secondarily "folk" or "people," as typically agricultural. In the same way Pali *kassaka*, "ploughman," and *kasi* or *kasī*, "ploughing," "tilth," are secondarily "farmer" and "folk." In many passages *pañca carṣaṇayaḥ* or *kṛṣṭayaḥ* replaces the more usual *pañca janāḥ*, for example R.V., V, 86, 2; VII, 15, 2; and IX, 101, 9, the first of these references giving us "Let us make oblation to Indrâgnī for sake of the Five Kindreds" (*pañca carṣaṇir-abhi*). Agni or Indra is *rāja* or *pati kṛṣṭīnām* or *carṣaṇīnām*, IV, 17, 5, and V, 39, 4, etc.,[7] and these expressions amount to the same things as *viśpati* elsewhere; Varuṇa is *rāja carṣaṇi-dhṛta*, king and supporter of the folk, IV, 1, 2; Agni takes his seat in homes as *gṛhapati* "for the sake of the Five Kindreds," *pañca carṣaṇir-abhi*, VII, 15, 2. Agni is himself *viśva-carṣaṇi*, V, 23, 4; the Buddha speaks of himself as *kassaka*, S.N., text I, p. 172.

It has often been observed that no trace of a caste system can be recognized in the *Ṛg Veda*. For example, the Creator *per artem* (Viśvakarma, Tvaṣṭṛ) is what would now be called a *śūdra*; and although the four characteristic functions of priest, ruler, farmer, and craftsman are distinguished, one and all of these are "ploughmen." What this implies is a state of affairs in which the individual of a given type is still in full possession of all the possibilities of being in the mode of that type. A caste system on the other hand reflects a posterior condition in which the individual realises in himself only a part of the potentialities that are proper to the type generically; "priest," "king," etc., are now *specific* determinations, the names alluding to the one and only function which the individual can properly fulfil, and which is his "vocation." As the process of contraction and identification into variety proceeds, the capacities of the individual are more and more constricted; and this is outwardly reflected in our contemporary social order (an industrial order representing the notion of "caste" in its fullest possible development), where none takes all knowledge for his province, and the workman is specifically conformed to the making of small parts of things and can make nothing whole. This excessive division of labour can result in the production only of goods that are useful, not of those that are beautiful; for integration, co-ordination, and lucidity are essential to beauty, and with these the labourer has nothing to do; he who makes only parts of things cannot be an artist (*artifex*) but only a cooly. Only those modern productions can be beautiful in which the products of the work of many men are united. If for example a bridge is beautiful, this is possible inasmuch as all those (engineer, and skilled and unskilled workers), who are collectively its maker, amount to one single proper man, one bridge-builder. Where a "tradition" has survived (as in "Campagnonage") it still remains within the power of the initiated individual to rise above the situation in which he finds himself, and by successive apperceptions to achieve a repossession of the lost powers; but this conception of the meaning of 'initiation into the mystery of a craft" has no longer any place in European consciousness. These considerations lie in part outside the natural limits of the present tract; but the fact that the *Ṛg Veda* recognises a state of affairs in which a division of labour is apparent only in act and not in the essence of the individual (the dual Indrâgnī, for example, represents the union of spiritual and temporal powers in one person, of which traces have survived in human social order wherever the links of tradition have not been broken) shows that we are here dealing with a "time" antecedent to "history."

THE ṚG VEDA AS LAND-NÁMA-BÓK

NAU

It will be seen below, (s.v. Sarasvatī) that the floor of the Chariot of Light (*jyoti-ratha* applied to Agni, Soma, Viśvedevāḥ, R.V., I, 140, 1; IX, 86, 44; X, 63, 4), that is of intellectual substance (*manas-maya*, X, 85, 2) and drawn by steeds not born of horses (*anaśvo jāto*, IV, 36, 1) but intellectually fashioned (*tatakṣur manasā*, I, 20, 2), is itself a Ground (*budhna*, X, 135, 6) resting upon the Waters, and in this respect like any other Earth (*pṛthivī* = *dyāvā-pṛthivī* = *dyāvā*) or platform of being. According to another familiar image any Ground may be represented by the lotus, flower or leaf, and it is in this sense (T.S., IV, 1, 4; IV, 2, 8; V, 2, 6, 5: ŚB., VII, 4, 1, 7-11) that Agni is said to have been churned from the lotus (*puṣkarāt*, VI, 16, 13) and *Vasiṣṭha*, child of Mitrâvaruṇau and Urvaśī, is born in the lotus (*jātaḥ . . . puṣkare*, VII, 33, 11) where also the Viśvedevāḥ are revealed.

Any Ground thus supported in and by the primordial ocean of infinite possibility may in the same way be thought of as a ship or ark (*nau*) or swing or rocking-boat (*prêṅkha*) of life, cf. *kṣauṇī-nau* in the invocatory stanzas of the *Daśakumāracarita*. So Vasiṣṭha, in Ṛ.V., VII, 88, when he feels himself estranged from Varuṇa—" My God, why hast thou forsaken me?"—looks back to the beginning with a fond yearning, as of Adam's for Paradise: " Where I with Varuṇa embarked (*ā ruhāva*), drave out our ship (*nāvam īrayāva*) into mid-ocean, rode on the crests of the waves, would that we yet swung there in the smooth-gliding swing (*prêṅkha*) for gladness, where-aboard (*nāvi*) Varuṇa set Vasiṣṭha, in the clear-shing of the days, when Heaven and Earth, the Dawns and Dusks were warped" (*tatanan*). " Wise King Varuṇa, indeed, made in Heaven this Golden Swing smooth-gliding for delight," VII, 87, 5; it is the Sun's reflection in the Sea, the " sun-boat " of the manifold tradition.

The Ship of Life may equally as well be spoken of as launched and guided by all or any of the premier Angels; thus, X, 63, 10, "Let us embark (*ā ruhema*) in the angelic vessel (*daivīṁ nāvam*) unto weal." Again, "The Ships of Truth (*satyasya nāvaḥ*) have borne the goodly-made across (*sukṛtam apīparan*, IX, 73, 1); "Bear us across the Sea as in a ship, thou Comprehensor" (*nāvā na sindhum ati parṣa vidvān*, IX, 70, 10, addressed to Soma; "As in a ship convey us o'er the flood" (I, 97, 8, addressed to Agni, cf. I, 99, i, "through peril as in a boat across a river"); "May we ascend the vessel of safe passage, whereby we may pass over manifold and grievous dangers" (VIII, 42, 3, addressed to the Angels collectively); "Transport us safely o'er manifold perils, ye Charioteers of the Law, as it were in ships across the Waters" (VIII, 83, 3); and "As in a ship o'er billows, so through divers states of being (*pradiśaḥ pṛthvyāḥ*, lit., "earthly regions," where as usual "earth" is any ground or platform of being); o'er manifold and grievous perils hath the Mighty Laud (*bṛhaduktha*, i.e., Agni) set (*ā adadhāt*) his children (*prajām*), by these and farther shores" (*avariṣu, pareṣu*, X, 56, 7). In J.B., I, 125 (see *J.A.O.S.*, XXVIII, 1, p. 84) the boat is a "ship-city" (*nau-nagara*), viz., that of the three-headed Gandharva (the Sun, cf. IX, 85, 12) that swims in the midst of the Waters, or as we should say in modern parlance, a great liner.

Often enough, according to another formulation, it is the Aśvins[8]—twins diversely born (R.V., I, 181, 4, and V, 73, 4), thus representing a principial duality essential to existence, and therefore naturally deliverers of things not yet in act, healers of all imperfect things[9]—who take up from the Waters into their living ships those that are not good swimmers, but are struggling in the Sea that is "without beginning or platform or any hold" (*anārambhāne . . . anāsthāne agrabhaṇe samudre*, I, 116, 5).[10] The Aśvins are the healers in particular of the aged

FIG. 2.—THE SHIP OF LIFE, OR SUN-BOAT, AND RIVER OF LIFE WITH ITS TWO SHORES. From an M.S. of the *Kalpa Sūtra* belonging to Mr. N. M. Heeramaneck, New York, see Brown, *Miniature paintings of the Kalpasūtra*, 1934, Fig. 30.

The miniature illustrates one of the Fourteen Dreams of Triśalā, all of which dreams, prefiguring the advent of Mahavira, are essentially the themes of the Creation as described in the *Ṛg. Veda*. "Every mother (*māyā* = *mātṛ*) of a Tīrthaṁkara sees these Fourteen Dreams in that night in which the most glorious Arhat enters her womb" (*Kalpa Sūtra*, § 46b). For a description of the River or Sea of Life as here depicted see *Kalpa Sūtra*, text 43, or translation in SBE., XXII, pp. 236–7, where the significant designations *gaṅgāvarta*, *uccalat* and *praty-avanivtta*, *kṣīra-sāgara*, and *salilam* are employed.

The "lookout" at the top of the mast is the Sun as the surveyor of all things (*viśvam abhi caṣṭe*, R.V., I, 164, 44, *abhicakṣana*, II, 40, 5, etc.), the mast his "foot" as Aja Ekapad, and at the same time, the Axis of the Universe, as pointed out explicitly in the *Daśakumāracarita*, invocatory verse, cf. my *Elements of Buddhist Iconography*, Note 139.

Cyavāna, who is or is in the likeness of Prajāpati, when overcome by eld (see s.v. Sarasvatī), and the saviours of Bhujyu (" Man " as the seeker of " enjoyment " or experience,[11] or possibly also as " serpent," *ante principium*).

The rescue of Bhujyu or other Prophets by the Aśvins from mid-ocean, and their safe return to port is referred to in R.V., I, 116, 3-5 ; I, 182, 5-7 ; I, 160, 3 and elsewhere. In the first of these passages we find " Ye brought him back in living ships (*ātmanvan-naubhiḥ*[12]), traversing mid-space (*antarikṣa*), above the waves . . . to the sea's strand (*samudrasya dhanvan*) . . . to his home (*astam*, cf. X, 14, 8, *punar astam ehi*), alive (*ātasthivāṅsam*, cf. from *sthā*, to be born, subsist, exist) on a ship " (*nāvam*. In I, 160, 3, the ship is called a ferry (*peru*) that is well equipped (*yukta*) and launched on the open sea (*madhye arṇaso dhāyi*) ; in I, 182, the ships, here four, are *ātmanvat* and winged (that is " angelic "), and there is also presented the alternative image of the Tree of Life (*vṛkṣa*) standing (*niṣṭhita*) in mid-ocean (*madhya arṇaso*) and to which the suppliant Bhujyu clings.[13]

The last passages recall the sky-faring ship of A.V., XIX, 39, 7-8, that is provided with a golden hawser (*bandhana*), and where for its passengers who " see life " (*amṛta*[14]) there is no slipping back again ;[15] the tree of R.V., I, 182, suggests that tree to which the ark of Manu is tied in Ś.B., I, 8, 1, 6. In any case it is clear that the pattern of the First Voyage is reflected in, and in principle identical with, that of the recurrent voyages of Manu, coincident with every minor *pralaya ;* for here, too, though from a lesser distance, the generative principles destined to prolong their line in the ensuing *manvantara* are carried over from the past and brought to land. It is to be noted too that the waters of the Flood rise and again in due time subside (just as in R.V., I, 164, 51, " uniformly with the days[16] this water rises up and falls away " (*uc ca ety ava ca*), and as to the subsidence, just as in III,

33, 10, the River "bows down like a nursing mother, yields like a maiden to her lover."

Now, so far as I know, it has never been propounded by any scholar, however historically minded, that the voyage of Manu, or for that matter, Noah's, represents the legendary memory of an historical migration.[17] *A fortiori*, in the case of the first of all voyages, it is a grave defect in understanding, to find in the Ship of Life no more than the reminiscence of some prehistoric Mayflower. What then becomes of the captain, and the passengers, the passage and the landfall ? Could any but the most naïvely profane (*pratyakṣa-priyā*) minds have seen here no more than the record of an ethnic Volkerwanderung, or map of a terrestrial geography ?

PAÑCA JANĀḤ, CARṢAṆAYAḤ, OR KṚṢṬAYAḤ

Indian sources are not absolutely unanimous as to the precise constitution of the Five Kindreds. It will suffice to cite the lists as given in A.B., III, 31, where we find *devāḥ, mānuṣyāḥ, gandharvâpsarasaḥ, sarpāḥ, pitaraḥ* (the Vaiśvadeva litany is proper to these Five), and *Bṛhad Devatā*, VII, 68, where we have *mānuṣyāḥ, pitaraḥ, devāḥ, gandharvāḥ, uraga-rākṣasaḥ*, or alternatively, *gandharvāḥ, pitaraḥ, devāḥ, asurāḥ, yakṣa-rākṣasaḥ*.[18] Without discussing the definition of these classes in detail, it may be remarked that even in these lists *mānuṣya* by means necessarily means " human " in a merely terrestrial sense, for many of the Angels, and particularly Agni and Indra, are often spoken of as manlike, that is to say as manifested and operating in the humane mode ; Indra, for example, is *nṛtama*, R.V., IV, 6, 4, and " the Spiritus (*prâṇa*) shines upon this world in the shape of a Person " (*puruṣa-rūpeṇa*, A.A., II, 2, 1) :[19] In any case the Ṛg Veda provides us with texts amply sufficient to prove that the Five Kindreds which participate in the First

Sacrifice are classes or categories of divine beings or principles, ancestors indeed of humanity, but not yet merely human in a biological sense. In R.V., X, 53, the Five Kindreds, *pañca janāḥ*, "who eat the Bread of Life" are summoned to cross Aśmanvatī, are also spoken of as a *daivya jana*, "Heavenly Kin," and as *yajñiyāsaḥ* "proper to be sacrificially worshipped," expressions that cannot have applied to living members of the genus Homo sapiens. In A.V., X, 7, 21, the Kindreds (*janāḥ*), sc. *pañca janāḥ*) having a superior understanding are contrasted with "those below" (*avare*) whose understanding is profane.[20] The Five Kindreds are furthermore synonymous with the ere-dwellers (*viśa*) and their rulers (*viśpati*); for "The dear Five have in the dear Light ere-begotten made-their-home" (*sam aviśanta*, R.V., X, 55, 2), and that is in Heaven (*divîva pañca kṛṣṭayaḥ*, X, 60, 4). All alike are prospered by the Sarasvatī (R.V., VI, 61, 12).

SARASVATĪ

In the Ṛg Veda, the act of creation is referred to under no aspect more fundamental than that of the release of the Waters (*āpaḥ*) that have been confined within the hollow-depths (*kha*) of the Rock or Mountain (*aśma*, *adri*, *budhna*, *himavat*) where Vṛtra holds them back. When the Waters are figuratively spoken of as Cows,[21] then the Mountain is the stony fold in which they are imprisoned. The release of the Waters or the Cows is also the Finding of the Hidden Light.[22] The Rock is likewise the birthplace of Agni (R.V., II, 12, 3), and thence he gets his chthonic (*budhnya*) steeds and other treasures (R.V., VII, 6, 7, and X, 8, 3). The Tree of Life is rooted in the same Ground (*budhna*, R.V., I, 24, 7).[23] The inexhaustible Well (*utsa akṣita*, R.V., VIII, 17, 16, elsewhere simply *utsa*, and sometimes *avata*) whence pours forth the River of Life, Sarasvatī, with her seven sister streams, is also the seat of Varuṇa, whose abode is "in the rivers' welling forth" (*sindhūnām upódaye*, R.V., VIII, 41, 8; there too is Agni's track (*utsasya madhye padaṁ veḥ*, X, 5, 1, cf. "the hidden treasure, as it were the Bird's germ in the Everlasting Rock," *aśmany anante*, I, 130, 3). If need were to justify the designation of Sarasvatī, or sometimes Aśmanvatī (obviously an essential name of the stream that flows from the Rock, *aśmano hy apaḥ prabhavanti*, Ś.B., IX, 1, 2, 4 = *śṛṇvantu āpaḥ . . . adreḥ*, R.V., V, 41, 12), as the River of Life (or in the plural when the seven sister rivers are mentioned), there can be referred to such expressions as "the Waters drenched (*sarayante*) the waste-lands" (*dhanvāni*), R.V., IV, 17, 2—the Grail motif—and more specifically "In thee, Sarasvatī, angelic, inheres every angelic life, grant unto us progeny" (*tve viṣvā sarasvatī śritā āyūṁsi devyān . . . prajāṁ devī didiḍḍhi naḥ*, R.V., II, 41, 17); again, the quality of maternity is constantly attributed to all or any of the "Rivers."[23a]

The Waters, thought of as enclosed and hidden, that is as they are in themselves and motionless, represent (as in all other traditions, e.g., Genesis) the infinite sum of all the possibilities of manifestation or non-manifestation. "This is the paradox, that when the Rivers flow (*caranti . . . nadyaḥ*), then are the Waters at a stand" (*tasthur āpaḥ*, R.V., V, 47, 5). The enigma is resolved when we take into account the meanings of root *sthā*, to be born, individualised, concrete, existent, or extant (ex-*stans*)[24]; principial motion *there*, is birth, concrete existence, *here*.

It will be familiar that in the Ṛg Veda the universe (*viśvam*, *bhuvanāni*, etc.) is thought of as expanded (root *pinv*, e.g., in X, 72, 7) from a middle point or centre, coincident with the centre of the world-wheel and the single source of Light, but thought of in our texts as a Ground, Rock, or Mountain (the Christian "Rock of Ages") in the midst of the primordial Ocean, and which would be an island could we think of such an all-pervading Sea as having a plane surface; it is here that all the potentiality of the In-finite (*aditi*) is as it were focussed, to flow in act for ever outward. This is the "birthplace of Order" (*ṛtasya yoni*) and the common Nest (*eka nīḍa*) wherein all the Angels and all creatures have been fledged.

So far as the River of Life flows eddying outwards thence,[25] so far are the possibilities of being realised within with the cosmic orb, so far is the verdure of the "waste-land" (*dhanva*) renewed, which "waste-land" or "desert" represents the latency of worlds not yet in being. "Where the Sarasvatī is lost" (*sarasvatyā vinaśane*, P.B., XXV, 10, 16) will be the outermost limit of the universe, the felly of the world-wheel. There on the banks of the River of Life, or as it were on Island-continents (*dvīpa*) representing "places where" the possibilities of being are severally realisable in indefinitely various modes, the Kindreds are "settled down" (*avasita*).

The occupation of the Light-world by the Kindreds thus implies a crossing over (root *tṛ*) of the River or Sea of Life by the cattle-loving people to a landfall "here."[26] References to the First Crossing of the River of Life are plenty in the Ṛg Veda. For example, "Here flows Aśmanvatī, hold fast together, stand up (*ut tiṣṭhata*, 'proceed,' that is, 'from potentiality to act'), my friends, and cross (*tarata*); let us abandon there the unkindly powers, let us cross over (*ut tarema*, 'disembark') to them that are propitious," R.V., X, 53, 8, where the crossing is of the Eight Ādityas and the Five Kindreds, cf. III, 33, where those that cross the "most maternal river" (*sindhu, vipāś*) are the cattle-loving Bharatas. In both cases the First Crossing is accomplished in the heavenly chariot (the Biblical "chariot of fire"), and in the latter the River, obedient to Viśvāmitra's incantation, so bends herself and sinks that the current flows no deeper than the axle-tree, "Your waves may touch the axle-pins (*śamyā*), but spare the traces" (III, 33, 13).[27] On making land, the pioneers take possession by the erection of a fire-altar, and from the ploughing that is requisite for this and for their own subsistence are called "ploughmen" or "farmers"[28]; "he ferried o'er the folk that might not swim (*asnātṝn apārayat*), and they having come ashore (*utsnāya*) attained to riches (*rayim* = Lat. *rem*), R.V., II, 15, 5, cf. VII, 60, 7.

SETU

The means of passage that links the Light- and Dark-worlds may also be conceived, not as a ship or chariot, but as a bridge or dyke (*setu*), which may be either easy (*suvita*) or hard to cross (*durāvya*, R.V., IX, 41, 2, the latter designation being the equivalent of "Brig o'Dread" in Scottish border ballads and Arthurian tradition): the bridge is originally crossed by the "Wise King," and is "his own" (*rājā . . . apaś ca vipras tarati sva-setuḥ*, R.V., X, 61, 16), being thus evidently a bridge of light, the pathway of the Sun. It is the Essence in its discriminative mode that separates the worlds (B.U., IV, 4, 22 and C.U., VIII, 4, 2).[28a] From the *jñāna kāṇḍa* point of view the bridge is a way *on*, or what is the same thing of *return* (in the positive sense), for example in K.U., III, 2, rather than of first coming forth; and this means that to walk upon it is the same thing as to continue in the ship of life on the angelic voyage (*devayāna*); hence it is called the "bridge of aeviternity" (*amṛtasya . . . setuḥ*, M.U., II, 2, 5), and it is said that neither day nor night, death nor sorrow, virtue nor vice can pass it, but only such as have the habit of the spiritual power (*brahmacarya*) can pass to and fro at will (*sarveṣu lokeṣu kāmâcāro bhavati*, C.U., VIII, 4, 3). This bridge is then the Wayfarer's pathway onwards to the Sun and through the Sun to the worlds of Varuṇa, the Fisher

King; it corresponds to the vertical of the Cross, the Gnostic *sthauros*, the trunk of the Tree of Life (cf. Jack and the Beanstalk), to the Ray that in early Christian nativities links the Bambino with the Supernal Sun, or in Mai. U., VI, 30, that one of the Sun's rays that rises aloft, piercing his disk, and extending to the Brahma-world.

It is just in this connection that we find in Grail tradition, viz., in Chretien's *Perceval* (section by Gautier) that the pathway by which Gawain reaches the Grail castle is a wave-washed causeway, which he crosses by night, guided rather by his horse than finding his own way; all of which is appropriate to his character of solar hero, the steed for example having been that of a slain knight who had been engaged upon the same quest, and properly the vehicle of the Sun, by which he proceeds. In Irish tradition it is the " Bridge of the Cliff " by which Cuchullain passes over from the bright world to the misty *dūn* of Scathach, from whom he learns wisdom and upon whose daughter he begets a son (whom he afterwards meets on earth and slays unawares in single combat, as did Sohrāb Rustum); along a part of the way to the bridge Cuchullain is borne on lion-back, and for another part is guided by a wheel; at last the " scholars of Scathach " point out the bridge, which is described as rising up and throwing back all who try to cross it; Cuchullain himself only succeeds at a fourth attempt (in connection with a solar hero this must mean at night), when he is " transfigured " and performs his " salmon-leap "—all details that can be readily understood, if we recall, for example, that the leap of a salmon is characteristically upstream, and especially against a fall of water, and is a return to its place of origin, and compare all this with the imagery of " inverse thinking " (*pratyak-cetanā*) as a going " up-stream " (*pratikūla*, *pratîpa*), cf. *Yoga Sūtra*, I, 29.[28b]

THE ṚG VEDA AS LAND-NÁMA-BÓK

VĀPA-MAÑGALA

A ploughing festival, or more strictly speaking "Feast of Seed-time," in which the king or headman plays the chief part, has been observed in India, and indeed throughout the world, as an indispensable agricultural ritual from time immemorial.[29] For example, in J., I, 57, "The king observed the Feast of Seedtime. On that day they adorn the town like the abode of the angels. . . . At such time the king takes hold of a golden plough (*naṅgala*, cf. *lāṅgala*), the attendant ministers a hundred and seven silver ploughs, the farmers (*kassaka*) the other ploughs. Holding them, they plough this way and that way. The king goes from one side to the other and back again." It is on this occasion that the miracle takes place of the staying of the sun above the Jambu tree under which the Bodhisattva has been laid by his father. This represents a "solstice," or more strictly speaking the turning point of the Spring equinox, the beginning of the Year, and at the same time the relation of the Comprehensor to the Supernal-Sun, as in C.U., III, 10, 4, where for one who has attained the state of Sādhya (= Muni), of Brahmā, the Sun "rises in the zenith and sets in the nadir"—and thus, as in the case of the miracle of the Jambu tree, casts no moving shadow.[30] Again in S.N., text I, 172, the farmer (*kasi*, "ploughman") Bhāradvāja (= the Vedic *ṛṣi* of that name) observes the Feast of Seedtime, and it is upon this occasion that the Buddha also names himself as "Ploughman" (*kassaka* = *karṣaka*).[31]

For the significance of the ploughing preparatory to the building of the fire-altar and the performance of the horse-sacrifice, cf. R.V., X. 101, 3-6 and IV, 57, 8 which may be conveniently cited as arranged with additions in T.S., IV, 2, 5 (Keith's version in H.O.S. 19, p. 315), "The sages yoke the ploughs; . . . here sow in the womb made ready the seed. . . . The plough, propitious

. . . plougheth up a cow, a sheep, and a fat blooming maid, a chariot support with a platform. With prosperity may our ploughs plough the ground. . . . The furrow annointed with ghee . . . do thou, O furrow, turn toward us with milk." The rite is more fully described in Ś.B., VII, 2, 2, 5, "it is for the seed that the womb (*yoni*) the furrow (*sītā*) is made," and 7, where it is made very clear that the ploughing, like the whole *yajña* which occupies the "year," is in imitation of what was done "in the beginning": "Ploughing means food (*annam vai kṛṣir-etad-vā*). It was when the Angels set-about-to-reintegrate (*saṁkariṣṭa*) Agni-Prajāpati," i.e. when he had been disintegrated by his act of generation (*sa prajāḥ sṛṣṭvā . . . vyasraṅsata . . . vīryam udakrāmat . . . apadyat*), "that they first put food into him (*purastād annam adadhuḥ*, where *purastād* is *agre, in principio*) and in like manner does this (Sacrificer) now when he sets about to accomplish his (Prajāpati's) reintegration, first put food into him."[32] Sixteen furrows are ploughed, defining the special directions; the ploughing is sunwise, avoiding a movement towards the south.

As regards the furrow, *sītā*, it will be recalled that in the *Rāmâyaṇa*, Ch. LXVI, Janaka's daughter is not in the usual way begotten: "As I was ploughing the mead, there arose a maid; and since I got her when hallowing the field, she has come to be known as the Furrow (*sītā*)." In this case the act of ploughing has itself a directly sexual significance, and in fact, the use of *kṛṣṭi*, lit. "that which is ploughed up" to mean "man," parallels the motion of the sexual act as a ploughing, implied in the notion of woman as a "field."[33] Compare also A.V., XI, 5, 12, "Roaring on, thundering, the ruddy-white goer (presumably Agni-Rudra) has introduced into the earth a great virile member; the Vedic student pours seed upon the surface, on the earth; thereby the four quarters live," and also the setting up of the

Hāṭakeśvara liṅgam in the bowels of the earth as related in the various versions of the Devadāruvana legend.[34]

VIŚA, VIŚPATI

Texts have already been cited in which the first settler or ere-dwellers, and their leaders and rulers are referred to as *viśa* and *viśpati*; the most important of these, R.V., X, 55, 2, having to do with the collective occupation (*sam-avasāna*) of the Light-world by the Five Kindreds. Such an occupation implies a procedure from darkness to light, interior to exterior operation, potentiality to act, *asuratva* (or *sarpatva*) to *devatva*. The ere-dwellers are immigrants, that have come forth in search of a home to dwell in, *īryur āviśam*, R.V., II, 24, 6, cf. A.V., VII, 41 (42), 1, where the Falcon (Agni[35]) "man-regarding" (i.e., for the sake of the Kindreds) "cleaves his way o'er waste and water, crossing all the nether spaces, looking for a home" (*avasāna-darśaḥ*). Agni is not only the forerunner (*pūrvam ārta*, R.V., IV, 1, 12, and "path-finder," *passim*) in this expedition, but a chieftain (*viśpati*, R.V., X, 4, 4 and X, 92, 1); or it may be Yama (who is in fact a particular aspect of Agni, cf. R.V., I, 164, 46) who finds a home for and unites the Kindreds, in the first place here in the worlds (R.V., X, 14, 2, *yamo no gātum prathamo viveda, na eṣā gavyutir apabhartavā u*, and 9, *ahobhir adbhir aktubhir vyaktaṁ yamo dadhāty avasānam asmai*, or again X, 18, 3 *yamaḥ sadanā te minotu*), and secondly there beyond.[36] So too in Ś.B., VII, 1, 1, 1 and 4, where it is clear that those are first settlers or ere-dwellers (*viśa*) who build a fire-altar on any land, the performance of this rite constituting the legal act of land-taking,[37] Yama is the ruler: "One settles (*avasyati*) when he builds the *gārhapatya*, and whoever are builders of fire-altars are 'settled' (*avasitāḥ*). . . . The Patriarchs (*pitaraḥ*) have made this world for him (*akrann imam pitaro lokam asmā*)[38]; Yama is the temporal power (*kṣatra*), and the Patriarchs the settlers (*viśāḥ*)."

As regards the setting up of the *gārhapatya*, it may be noted that the actual site is determined by casting eastward or forward (and subject to this condition, evidently at random) a yoke—or axle-pin (*śamyā*), as prescribed in P.B., XXV, 10, 4 and 13, 2. There is an allusion to this practice in S.N., text I, p. 76, where we find the expression *sammāpāsam*, "peg-thrown site."

YAJÑA

It is that there may be Light that the First Sacrifice is undertaken by the desirous Angels and Five Kindreds: "when the Five sacrificed to Agni" (V.S., XII, 23) that was as if to say "Come forth, for Man (*manu*) is angel-minded, fain to sacrifice," etc. (R.V., X, 5, 1). It was in fact "by means of this Session (*sattra*) that Agni came into the state of setting all things in motion" (*sarvasya prāsravaṇam agacchat*), or alternatively, thereby that Prajāpati[39] "stupified by age (*jīryyā mūra*), threw off his decrepitude (*jarām apāhata*) and came into the state of setting all things in motion," and so too "by means of this Session that Mitrāvaruṇau obtained these worlds" (P.B., XXV, 9, 2; 10, 10; and 17, 2 and 3). We must assume also that the "Serpent-Session" (*sarpa-sattra*) formed an essential, and indeed a first stage in the performance of the whole rite, for it was "thereby that the Serpents gained a firm support in these worlds (*eṣu lokeṣu pratyatiṣṭhan*), thereby that they vanquished Death (the state of mere potentiality, *ante principium*), changing their skins and creeping farther" (*hitvā jīrṇān tacam ati sarpante*), to be manifested in full act as the Ādityas, for the Ādityas are (a transformation of) the Serpents" (P.B., XXV, 15, 2 and 4).[40]

FIG. 3.—THE KINDLED FIRE OF THE FIRST SACRIFICE: "Fire that was made to flare upon the Rock," R.V., II, 24, 7. From a MS. of the *Kalpa Sūtra* belonging to Mr. N. M. Heeramaneck, New York, see Brown, *Miniature paintings of the Kalpasūtra*, 1934, fig. 33.

The miniature illustrates one of the Fourteen Dreams of Triśalā, see the description of our Fig. 2. For the description of this dream see the *Kalpa Sūtra*, text §46, in which the significant terms *ujjvala* and *madhu-ghṛta* may be noted; and translation, SBE., XXII, p. 238.

The First Sacrifice has been referred to above in the singular, it will however be understood that this is in a collective sense, the sacrifice actually consisting of many parts and distinct celebrations. In any case, it is "by means of this thousand years Session that the All-Emanators (*viśvasṛjaḥ*, i.e., all the powers participating in the act of creation) emanated all the Universe (*viśvam asṛjanta*), P.B., XXV, 18, 1-2.

The occasion of the First Sacrifice—*janā yad agnim ayajanta pañca*, V.S., XII, 23—is *agre*, *in principio*, at the beginning of an aeon, the birthday of the Supernal-Sun, the Springtide of the Cosmic Year, when "Dawn first shone for Man (*uṣāḥ uvāsa manave*, R.V., X, 5, 3), when "the doors of the worlds to come open for you with their months and years," and "ancient are all these things" (R.V., II, 24, 5). Its place is on that farther shore, which is also the rocky source of Sarasvatī-Aśmanvatī, from which the Argonauts go forth to find a home (*āviśam*), when once the cosmic beacon has been lit, "they left behind the Fire that by their arms was made to flare upon the Rock" (*te bāhubhyāṁ dhamitam agnim aśmani . . . jahuḥ*, R.V., II, 24, 7). When landfall is made, the settler's first concern is to establish the like ritual on "earth," that is on the banks of the River of Life, "where the Sarasvatī ends" (*sarasvatyā vinaśane*, i.e., where the waters meet the shores of the habitable worlds, cf., R.V., IV, 17, 2, *dhanvāni sarayante āpāḥ*); it is "forty days' journey thence upstream on horseback" to the Source (*śaiśava*), which is in fact the Fountain of Life, and "so far is Heaven from Earth," P.B., XXV, 10,1 and 16.[41]

It needs no argument to prove that the ritual on earth is performed in imitation of the First Sacrifice; "the observance of the rule thereof is the same as at the creation" (Ś.B., XIV, 1, 2, 26, and *passim*), and "in like manner does he, the sacrificer, even now" (Ś.B., VII, 2, 2, 7).[41a] The sacrifice, undertaken merely as *karma*, establishes the sacrificer securely where he is, it forms so to say his legal title to the taken land (Ś.B., VII, 1, 1, 1 and 4), and this significance suffices for an exegesis of the *mantras* regarded strictly as *karma kāṇḍa*, the point of view with which we are here mainly concerned. But is clear also that for "him who understands" (*ya evaṁ vidvān*) there is implied not merely a taking possession of these worlds, but a symbolic fulfilment of the sacrificer's whole course, a symbolical journeying to the Fountain of Life upstream, "to find there a full katharsis" (*avabhṛtam abhivedya*),[42] P.B., XXV, 10, 18. *Avabhṛta*, in ritual technique, is an "expiatory bath concluding the ceremony." In C.U., III, 17, where the whole course of life is interpreted in sacrificial terms, death as the concluding ceremony of the ritual is the *avabhṛta*. In the same way, an ablution in the Fountain of Life is a death, man's last end; for *avabhṛta* is also (and more literally) a "sinking down," as of foam into water, a "drowning," and in this profounder sense, the going down into the waters of the Fountain of Life is a descent "into the depths, into the well-spring of the Godhead" (Eckhart). Otherwise expressed, the sacrifice is said to be concluded "when the *gṛhapati* dies"; and where Agni is understood to be the *gṛhapati*, this will mean that the last end of life is attained when the flame of life is extinguished and despirated (*nirvāta*). That this last death of the soul is a passage out of our mortality into the pleroma (*kṛtsna*, *pūrṇa*) is implied by the apparently materialistic words of the text (P.B., XXV, 10, 18) when it is said that "there the sacrificer's hundred kine become a thousand" that is to say that once and for all he comes into effective repossession of all the potentialities of his being.

THE ṚG VEDA AS LAND-NÁMA-BÓK

YAMA AS VIŚPATI

" Yama first found the Way for us, this pasture never shall be taken from us " (R.V., X, 14, 2). The greater part of the wording of the " funeral hymns " of the Ṛg. Veda—considered apart from their actual application in funeral ceremonial, discussed below—has reference to Yama as pathfinder and gatherer together and ruler of " men " here in the Light-world; his connection with the Patriarchs is as their guide and leader on the road that leads to the so much desired extension of their " line," he is the patron of those travellers on the *pitṛyāna*, that is to say of those individual potentialities, whose course is hitherward, and only later hence. In X, 14, 8, the comer-on is exhorted to " Put away the curse, seek again thy home, and shining bright, assume a body " (*hitvā avadyam punar astam ehi, saṁ gacchasva tanvā suvarcāḥ*), where a reincarnation, not in the later and more literal (Buddhist) sense, but of the progenitive principles at the dawn of a new creation is implied. Cf. X, 58, surely not " an address to recall the fleeting intellect (*manas*) of a man at the point of death " (Griffiths), but to bring back an intellect at the appointed time *for birth*.[43]

Yama's brindled " Dogs " (no doubt the Sun and Moon, " four-eyed " inasmuch as they behold the four Quarters) that ward the Path are " man's " protectors against demoniac powers, the wolf (*vṛka*) and such; as " man-regarding,"[44] these " Dogs " can be identified with the " man-regarding spies " of R.V., IX, 73, 5-6, who " turn back the blind and deaf (for indeed) they that are malformed do not pass over on the Pathway of the Law " (*ṛtasya panthāṁ na taranti duṣkṛtaḥ*). The deformed, unformed, are turned back not merely as such, but are repelled also for the sake of " men," the principles of the Dark-world being necessarily, from the dualistic point of view of the *karma kāṇḍa*, thought of as hostile (*aśiva, śatru, ārāti*) to those of the Light-world; such indeed is the eternal opposition of Asura and Deva as it is envisaged from the mundane point of view.

What is the significance of this exclusion of the blind and deaf, or otherwise malformed? To be blind and deaf is the same as to be unawakened, unintelligent, and stupid (*abudhyamāna, acetasa, mūra*), devoid of any "human intellect" (*nṛmanas*) such as Agni's is. This is the condition of *sarpattva*,[45] cf. Ahi-Vṛtra *abudhyam, suṣupāṇam, āśayānam*, R.V., IV, 19, 3; and Agni's, as Ahi Budhnya, *ante principium*, cf. *apād aśīrṣā guhamāno antā*, R.V., IV, 1, 11, followed by *pra ārta* in the next verse, and A.B., III, 36, where it is stated that Ahi Budhnya is metaphysically (*parokṣeṇa*) what Agni Gārhapatya is outwardly (*pratyakṣa*), cf. Ahi Budhnya as the "old" and Aja Ekapād (the Sun) as the "new" *gārhapatyā*, P.B., I, 4, 11-12. With the injunction to the comer-on, *hitvā avadyam . . . vi sarpata atas*, etc., in X, 14, 9, compare P.B., XXV, 15, where the Serpents, "vanquishing Death (*mṛtyum ajayan*) casting their shrivelled skins (*hitvā jīrṇān tacam*) and creeping farther (*ati sarpanti*) become Ādityas," and so in his case who imitates their rite, "he too becomes a shining as of these Ādityas."[46]

"In the beginning . . . Death" (*mṛtyu*) not yet essentialised (*ātmanvī*, B.U., I, 2, 1)—neither sees nor hears, for he has neither Intellect nor Word nor Eye nor Ear, he is "incomplete" (*akṛtsna*, B.U., I, 4, 17); the yonder Brahman, not subject to mortality (*amarta*), is not-in-any-likeness (*amūrta*), B.U., I, 2, 1, and II, 3. In the same way it is said that "He is impotent (*starīḥ*) on the one hand and virile (*sūtaḥ*) on the other. He shapes his aspect as he wills," R.V., VII, 101, 3. That is to say that he is "impotent" in the dark night of time, in the "house of darkness" (*tamasi harmye*), and hence the designation of this state as Privation (*aśanāyā*) and Death (*mṛtyu*), B.U., I, 2, 1. This state of Privation is necessarily conceived from an empirical point of view (that of the human-animal, *paśu*, "whose discrimination is merely by hunger and thirst," *aṣanā-pipāse eva abhivijñānam*, A.A., II, 3, 2)[47] as a condition of pain, as for example in R.V., I, 105, where Agni's sufferings as Trita Āptya "in the Pit" (*kūpe*) are described.[48]

But now the Hidden Light is found and freed, there is a Harrowing of Hell, the incomplete are made whole: "when thou hast made him viable (*śritam*), O Jātavedas,[49] then speed him to the Patriarchs forth (*pra hiṇutāt pitṛbhyaḥ*), bear him to the world of the well-made (*sukṛtām*, opposed to *duṣkṛtaḥ* in IX, 73, 6, cited above). . . . Agni, re-emanate him (*ava sṛja punaḥ*) who now that thou has summoned him proceeds with his intrinsic-powers (*yas ta āhūtaś carati svadhābhiḥ*); induing life, let him proceed *in statu pupillaris* (*śesaḥ*, Sāyaṇa *śiṣyamāṇah*); what wound soever the blackbird, the ant, the snake, or jackal has inflicted, do thou Agni, all-devourer, heal, and Soma too, who bideth with the Brahmans," R.V., X, 16, 1-6.[50]

On the other hand, the application of the texts in a reverse sense is perfectly legitimate, recurrent death being in its turn a passage to another world, another life though still within the worlds; in R.V., X, 58, Yama is evidently the ruler of the dead in this sense. An ambiguity of application is inevitable,[51] if only because an extroversion must imply (wherever the cosmic process is conceived of as cyclic, *kreislaufig*), a corresponding and analogous introversion. It is in just the same way for example, that the revolution of the solar wheel, which from the *karma kāṇḍa* point of view is unto life in the worlds, becomes in *jñāna kāṇḍa* and in Buddhism a revolution unto death, the last death of the soul. There cannot be spiration without a corresponding despiration (*nir-vāṇa*). Most of the texts with which we are concerned have primarily to do with the *pitṛyāna*, the "Way of the Patriarchs." It is only those whose voyaging is sooner or later on the *devayāna*, the "Way of the

Angels," that make land again there where the coming forth and going in are not alternate, but one and the same thing; it may be said only of the Comprehensor, as of Agni, that "He proceedeth foremost, while yet abiding in his Ground" (*anu agrañ carati kṣeti budhnaḥ*, R.V., III, 55, 7).

Though Yama's is the dreaded path of death (R.V., I, 38, 5) and Agni is the very principle of life (*āyu*, *ekâyu*, *viśvâyu*, passim), the *Ṛg Veda* either identifies Yama with Agni (I, 164, 46), or calls the latter Yama's darling friend (*kāmya*, X, 21, 5) or priest (*hotṛ*, X, 52, 3), and there is a significant aspect in which their functions coincide, viz., as "gatherer together of the kindreds" (in I, 59, 1, Agni *janān . . . yayantha*, in X, 14, 1, Yama is *saṁgamano janānām*), cf. *ekam bhū*, "to become one," i.e., "to die." The contrasted functions are in fact united in the Golden Germ "whose likeness is that of life, and likeness that of death" (X, 121 2), in the Year "that separates some beings and unifies others" (AĀ., III, 2, 3). How these two that are the same play into each other's hands can be seen in R.V., I, 163, 2-3, where the sacrificial horse (given to Death by Agni as priest and sacrificial fire of the Aśvamedha) is given by Yama in turn to Trita, that is to Agni himself *ab intra*, is yoked by Trita, ridden by Indra, and identified with Yama, Varuṇa (*āditya*), and Trita. All these are One for the Comprehensor, absolutely unified (*ekadhā bhūtvā*, B.U., V, 5, 12), that is, dead and buried in the Godhead. We may say then that that it is as Yama that the dying man beholds Agni when he reaches the realm of the two kings, Yama and Varuṇa (X, 14, 17); and that for the Comprehensor (*vidvān*), and for any man that has done well, that one principle that some desire as life and others fear as death can be seen in either aspect as the Friend (*mitra*), the Meeting-place (*saṁgamana*), and Lord of the Settlers (*viśpati*); for him the paths of Agni and of Yama are one and the same *devayāna*.

CONCLUSION

It has been sought to show that the Ṛg Veda is not concerned with events in time, but with the "entering in of time from the halls of the outer heaven," that is *agre*, in the beginning, *in principio*. Nor can that entering in of time be thought of as itself an event in time; it is "first" and a "beginning" only in logical order of thought. Life is "crossing over" all the time, "out of the everywhere into here" and a motion forward to the "last end" (*puruṣârtha, param padam*).[52] *Sicut erat in principio, est nunc, et semper erit, in scæula sæculorum.* These are, of course, Pūrva Mīmāṁsaka points of view; but here they have been independently developed.

Some have been impressed by the "bewildering variety" of Indian mythology, ritual, and art: it would be nearer the truth to speak of its sameness or monotony,[53] for in fact it never departs from the fundamental theme of the Beginning of All Things (*jāta-vidyā*). And this is true in an even wider application, for this story of the first beginning, which also points the way to the last end, has been told in what is essentially one and the same way, although with abundant dialectic variation, throughout the world and from time immemorial, and survives even to-day not only in accepted scriptures, but also in fairy tale and nursery rhyme, and in folk art.

NOTES

[1] Jeremias, *Der Kosmos von Sumer*, 1932, p. 20.

[2] Cf. Andræ, *Die Ionische Säule; Bauform oder Symbol?* Berlin, 1933, pp. 65, 66: "When we sound the archetype, the ultimate origin of the form, then we find that it is anchored in the highest, not the lowest. . . . He who marvels that a formal symbol can remain alive not only for millennia, but that, as we shall yet learn, can spring to life again after an interval of thousands of years, should remind himself that the power from the spiritual world, which forms one part of the symbol, is everlasting." Cf. René Guénon, "Du prétendu 'empirisme' des ancients," in *Le Voile d'Isis*, No. 175, 1934.

[3] Abbreviations are employed as follows: R.V., *Ṛg Veda Saṁhitā*; A.V., *Atharva Veda Saṁhitā*; T.S., *Taittirīya Saṁhitā*; V.S., *Vājasaneyi Saṁhitā*; T.B., *Taittirīya Brāhmaṇa*; P.B., *Pañcaviṁśa Brāhmaṇa*; A.B., *Aitareya Brāhmaṇa*; J.B., *Jaiminīya Brāhmaṇa*; J.U.B., *Jaiminīya Upaniṣad Brāhmaṇa*; A.A., *Aitareya Āraṇyaka*; B.U., *Bṛhadāraṇyaka Upaniṣad*; C.U., *Chāndogya Upaniṣad*; Mai. U., *Maitri Upaniṣad*; M.U., *Muṇḍaka Upaniṣad*; S.N., *Samyutta Nikāya*; J., *Jātaka*.

[4] "The Comprehensors (*vidvāṅsaḥ*) . . . they of the Law (*ṛtavānaḥ*, here the First Sacrificers) when they had bared to sight what-things-were-theirs-who-knew-no-Law (*anṛtā*), and were returned, they, the shaper-minstrels (*kavayaḥ*, Gk. ποιηταί went forth upon their glorious way," R.V., II, 24, 6-7; "The Patriarchs (*pitaraḥ*), on whom as being Angels, the Angels have bestowed their Providence (*kratu*) . . . have overstridden the regions, laying out the ancient measureless abodes . . . pouring out their offspring variously," X, 56, 4-5; "The generous (viz., *viśvedevāḥ*) have made the Sun to mount the sky, and scattered the Aryan ordinances (*āryā vratā*) o'er the world," X, 65, 11 (Sāyaṇa glosses *ārya* as *śreṣṭhāni* and *kalyāṇāni*, "best" and "lovely"). *Per contra*, "The Herdsman of the Law (*ṛtasya gopā*), the Comprehensor who surveys the several worlds (viz., the Sun), thrusts into the pit them that are unqualified (*ajuṣṭān*) and uninitiate (*avratān*). Men of vision (*dhīraḥ*, here the First Sacrificers) span the yarn of Law (*ṛtasya tantur vitataḥ*) upon the purifying sieve, Varuṇa's tongue-tip, by Magic (*māyayā*); but he that is not able thereunto (*aprabhuḥ*) falls down into the pit (*kartam ava padāti*), R.V., IX, 73, 9; mark the contrast as between the latter and the "Herdsman moving on the paths, who never falls" (*gopām anipadyamānam . . . pathibiś carantam*, I, 164, 31 and X, 177, 3, J.U.B., III, 37). The Herdsman of the Universe (*bhuvanasya gopā*, I, 164, 21, II, 27, 4, VII, 70, 2, J.U.B., I, 1, and III, 12, etc.) is the "Good shepherd" of Semitic tradition. Indra is typically designated *vratapā*, Fidei Defensor, which is his natural function as representing the temporal power (*kṣatra*) in alliance with the spiritual-power (*brahma*) represented by Agni, who lays the bolt in Indra's hands, X, 52, 5, and appoints him to perform heroic feats, VIII, 100, 1-2.

[5] In R.V., IV, 1, 7, where Agni is *arya*, Sāyaṇa's gloss is *svāmi vaiśyayor*, tantamount to "*viśpati*."

[6] Cf., however, Namuci's reproaches addressed to Indra, "Thou betrayer of a friend," T.B., I, 7, 1, 7-8. There is indeed plenty of evidence in the *Ṛg Veda* that the act of taking possession of what was not originally theirs, but belonged to the dusky Asuras—as if to the "Redskins" in our American analogy—was well understood to have been in some sort a sin requiring expiation and a symbolic restitution, e.g., R.V., X, 109; the *kilbiṣāṇi* are typically Indra's, while the Redeemer, *kilbiṣa-spṛt*, is typically Agni, R.V., X, 71, 10; it may also be noted with respect to R.V., I, 164, 32, where Agni is said to "take on destruction" (*nirṛtim*), that if we accept Sāyaṇa's designation of Nirsti as *pāpa-devatā*, this also implies an assumption of our guilt. We are not, however, at present concerned with this point of view, but only with that affirmative attitude which naturally prevails in the *karma kāṇḍa*.

[7] In R.V., I, 177, 1, Indra, and in III, 62, 6, Bṛhaspati, is *vṛṣabha carṣaṇinām*.

[8] The origin of the Aśvins "is to be sought in a pre-Vedic period . . . (they) may originally have been conceived as finding and restoring or rescuing the vanished light of the sun" (Macdonell, *Vedic Mythology*, pp. 49, 51, cf. von Schröder, in W.Z.K.M., IX, 131).

[9] R.V., X, 39, 3: "Ye are the gladness of her that groweth old at home (unwed), furtherers of him that hath no horse and lags behind, healers of the blind, the wasted and the broken." Cf. Ś.B., IV, 1, 5, 16: "The Aśvins are outwardly (*pratyakṣam*) these two, viz., Heaven and Earth, for it is these that have obtained possession of all things here. They are called the "lotus-crowned"; Agni is verily the lotus of this earth, the Sun of yonder sky." The ontological implications are evident; Heaven and Earth are healers of all things in that they provide the necessary basis of operation in one or other of the contrasted modes, terrestrial or celestial. The Aśvins inwardly (*parokṣeṇa*) are, no doubt, the brothers, "mortal and immortal," Mitrāvaruṇau, or Agni and Varuṇa, 1, 164, 30 and 38, and X, 85, 18.

From the *karma kāṇḍa* point of view release (*mokṣa*, root *muc*) is a setting free of potentialities *unto operation* (R.V., I, 112, 8, the Aśvins release (*amuñcatam*) the swallowed quail; I, 140, 4, Agni's steeds are *mumukṣaḥ*, as in X, 111, 9, the Rivers of Life are *mumukṣāṇāḥ*; V, 81, 2, the Sun as *kavi, viśvā rūpāṇi prati muñcate*, cf. I, 42, 1, where Pūṣan is *vimuco napāt*; VII, 59, 2, *bandhanāt mṛtyor mukṣīya na amṛtāt*); but from the *jñāna kāṇḍa* point of view, a release *from operation* (the latter sense is naturally rare in R.V., but cf. V, 46, 1, where *vimucam* and *āvṛttam punaḥ* are contrasted). In Buddhism, the concept of the Tathāgata as the finder of a medicine for eld and death (*jarā-maraṇa*) can only be regarded as an adaptation (*upāya*) to later mundane circumstances of the older concept of the Messiah as accomplishing with his awakening (Gautama, *buddha* = Agni, *uṣarbudh*) the Harrowing of Hell, cf. J., I, 76, *cakkavālantaresu . . . ekobhāsā ahesuṁ . . . jaccandhā rūpāṇi passiṁsu, jātibhadirā saddaṁ suniṁsu, jātipīṭhasappī padasā gacchiṁsu, andubandhanādīni chinditvā patiṁsu*, "There shone One Light throughout the voids-between-the-worlds (i.e., hells, in terms of space rather than of time), the naturally blind beheld the shapes of things, the naturally deaf heard sounds, the naturally halt went forth afoot, all bars and bonds were broken and fell away."

10 This Sea is the fathomless abyss, covered over by darkness, fluid and indeterminate, of R.V., X, 129. Cf. Augustine, *Confessionum*, XIII, 5, "the dark abyss, dark as regards the inconstant flux of its spiritual formlessness" (*informitas*), where the Waters, as in Genesis and R.V., are undetermined substance, infinite but mere potentiality, *ante principium*; and *ib.* XIII, 7, "waters devoid of any standing ground" (*sine substantia*), where by a natural extension of meaning, and just as also typically in Buddhism, the abyss is the inconstant sea of life, with all its dangers, and its imperfections now (*post principium*) to be regarded as deformities, that is to say now as partial rather than as before a total privation of form and being. The Sea to be passed over is continuous and unsubstantial (as Augustine so well expresses it, *loc. cit.*, "neque enim loca sunt, quibus mergimur et emergimus"); the end to be reached is that of a full and conscious possession of its own intrinsic form (*svarūpa*) by each and every individual potentiality that has been thought of as taking passage in the ship of life. The voyage once begun is not at an end when any given port is reached, but is onward by the *devayāna* to a port beyond our understanding, or by the *pitṛyāna* to and fro from port to port.

11 From the *karma kāṇḍa* point of view, the Ship of Life is built and oared for transport by the First Sacrifice (R.V., X., 101, 2); but from that of the *jñāna kāṇḍa*, "the sacrificial forms are unsafe boats," *Muṇḍaka Upaniṣad*, I, 2, 7, and it is in the vessel of the spiritual-power (*brahma*) that the Comprehensor should pass over all the fearful rivers," *Śvetāśvatāra Upaniṣad*, II, 8.

12 *Ātmanvat* is "hypostasised," and "conscious," cf. *sarvātmanvat*, A.V., X, 8, 2; *ātmanvat yakṣa*, the human self or essence, *ib.* X, 3, 43; *ātmanvī* in B.U., I, 2, 1.

13 In accordance with another formulation, beings dwelling in the Light-world, although fledglings of one nest (*viśo . . . santīḷaḥ*, R.V., I, 69, 3) and due to be reunited there at last (*yatra viśvam bhavaty ekanīḷam*, R.V., *khila*, IV, 10, 1, and V.S., XXXII, 8), are individually nested in the branches of the Tree of Life, cf. P.B., XI, 15, 1, "Nest (*kulāya*) is offspring, nest is cattle, nest is dwelling," and R.V., III, 54, 5-6, *avamā sadāṅsi . . . sadanaṁ yathā veḥ*.

14 "Life," rather than "immortality," cf. Hopkins in *J.A.O.S.*, XXVI, p. 37, "long life without decrepitude prior to expected death." The best rendering of *amṛta*, as attributed to *devas*, would be "æviternity," which is "a mean between eternity and time," see St. Thomas, *Sum. Theol.*, I q. 10, a. 5; angels are measured by time as regards their affections and intelligences, which are changeable; by æviternity as regards their nature; and as regards the vision of glory possess a share of eternity.

15 *Na avaprabhraṁśana*, where *avaprabhraṁśana* = *avasarpaṇa* in Ś.B., I, 8, 1, 7. Regarding the prefix *ava*, literally "down" though rendered above by "back again," observe that the coming forth hitherward is always expressed in terms of upward movement (verbal forms with prefix *ut* or *upa*), or what amounts to the same thing, forward (*arvāñc*) or eastward (*pūrvam*) movement. Coming into existence is an ascent, emergence, rising up (*ārohaṇa*, as opposed to *pratyañc* in R.V. *passim*, A. V., XIX, 6, 4, and J.U.B., I, 36) from potentiality to act. A backsliding (*avasarpaṇa*) into a state of non-being, the "pit" out of which we were digged, is from the incarnate standpoint *summum malum*; nevertheless a return from existence

to non-being when effected positively by way of integration (*saṁskaraṇa*) is from the intellectual or spiritual point of view the *summum bonum*. That backsliding and integration can both be spoken of as movements of *de*scent or *im*mersion must be understood in this sense, that whereas potentiality assumes the aspect of an evil when *contrasted* with act, all is " good " in the Supreme Identity where there is no distinction of potentiality from act. In other words, we come forth as those who cannot swim (*asnātṛ*) and return as accomplished swimmers (*snātṛ*) at home in any waters. These conceptions underlie the Christian and other symbolisms of the Redeemer as Fish, and of the redeemed as little fishes, cf. Tertullian, *De Bapt.*, I, " But we, little fishes (*pisciculi*) after the example of our *ΙΧΘΥΣ*, Jesus Christ, are born in water, nor have we safety in any other way than by permanently abiding in the water " ; baptism (and all the more when there is total immersion) prefiguring salvation ; for those whom the inundation of the world at the close of an aeon (at the " Judgment Day ") will not be liable to hurt are precisely those who are good swimmers. And in the same way Rūmī, " I am a great fish, and desire the Ocean of Omān " (XVI, in Nicholson, *Shams-i-Tabrīz*).

[16] " Days " here somewhat as in Genesis, and possibly already in the sense of *æons*. The notion of temporal hierarchies was no less familiar to the ancients than was that of spacial hierarchy, cf. Jeremias, *Handbuch der altorientalischen Geisteskultur*, p. 295 f. At the same time and inasmuch as all extension whether in time or space is in principle one and the same thing, the daily ebb and flow of oceanic tides, exposing and again submerging a strand (*dhanva*) is a reflection, analogy, or trace (*vestigium pedis* in the Scholastic sense, Skr. *pada*, see my *Elements of Buddhist Symbolism*, Note 146) of the subsidence and welling up of the fountains of the earth at the beginning and end of every cosmic " Day."

[17] A stranding on the summit of Himālaya would ill accord with any theory of a migration across the Indus. A landing on the summit of Mt. Ararat can hardly have been an historical event.

[18] Cf. the similar list of those who are carried by the cosmic stallion (whose kin and place are the primordial ocean), B.U., I, 1, 2 ; viz., *devāḥ, gandharvāḥ, asurāḥ*, which with addition of *pitaraḥ* would complete a tale of Five Kindreds. Incidentally, there can be recognized here the prototype of Avalokiteśvara as a saviour from shipwreck and patron of mariners, as for example in the *Valāhassa Jātaka*, cf. Goloubew, " Le Cheval Balāha," B.É.F.E.O., 1927, p. 235 f.

[19] Keith has observed that A.A., II, 2, " shows that the names of the seers of the Ṛg Veda can be deduced from *prāṇa's* actions " ; in other words, the seers are not " individuals " (but seven rays of Agni's Light, cf. R.V., II, 5, 2, and X, 62, 5-6).

Indra's associates in the First Foray are constantly referred to as " men " (e.g., R.V., IV, 1, 15, *naraḥ uṣijaḥ*). The " human " (*manuṣvat*) Agni as eighth Āditya " impels the whole angelic-operation " (*daivyam . . . viśvam invati*, R.V., II, 5, 2). Agni has " man's intellect " (*nṛmanaḥ*, R.V., X, 45, 1 and 2, that is effectively, " human nature "), cf. Eckhart, I, 236, citing " philosophers " to the effect that " human nature has nothing to do with time," and St. Thomas, *Sum. Theol.*, I, q. 3, a. 3, " This flesh, these bones, and the accidental qualities distinguishing this particular matter, are not included in humanity . . . humanity and a man are not wholly identical ; but humanity is taken to mean the formal part of man." This *forma humanitatis nunquam perit* (Thierry of Chartres). Vedic *narya* is tantamount to *daivya* as distinct from *asurya*. The *devas* are man-kin by what is common to angels and men, viz., intellect (*manas*), but are not therefore "men." Whereas of the *asuras* (who are *devas* in *potentia*) we may say that their nature is informal, unkind (un-kin), and uncouth or uncanny, using the latter words in their basic sense of "racially alien" and "unknowable" (that which is informal being *ipso facto* unknowable). In any case the Vedic usage of man and manly, or human, in no way proves that the references are anywhere to Homo sapiens of the taxonomist.

[20] The terms of the contrast suggest that the Kindreds are in possession of a wisdom handed down by initiatory transmission (*guru-paramparā*), which would be characteristic for "Aryans."

[21] The ownership of cows is the effective possession or realization of the possibilities of one's being, and it is from this point of view that the "eager men" who under Indra's leadership break through the stony barriers of the imprisoned kine are spoken of as "cattle-minded," or "cattle-bent" (*gavyanta*, IV, 17, 16, *gavyan grāmaḥ*, III, 33, 11, *gavyatā manasā*, IV, 1, 15, cf. s.v. *Yajña*, the hundred that become a thousand when the whole course of the sacrifice has been fulfilled).

[22] References for the statements summarized above are too numerous to be cited here in full. The following are typical: R.V., I, 56, 5, *yan mada indra harṣy āhan vṛtram nir apām aubjo arṇavam*; I, 62, 3, Bṛhaspati *bhinad adrim . . . vidad gāh*; I, 130, 3, *nihitaṁ guhā nidhiṁ ver na garbham . . . aśmany anante*; II, 12, 3, Indra *jajāna agnim aśmanor antaḥ*; II, 16, 3, Indra *vajreṇa khāni atṛṇan nadīnām*; IV, 3, 11, *ṛtena adriṁ vi . . . bhidanta . . . aṅgirasaḥ*; V, 41, 12, *śṛṇvantv āpaḥ . . . adreḥ*; X, 89, 4, *apaḥ . . . sagarasya budhnāt*; X, 113, 4, Indra *avṛścad adrim . . . ava sasyadaḥ sṛjat*.

[23] Inasmuch as the Tree of Life is rooted in and the River or Rivers of Life originate in one and the same Ground or Mountain (cf. Soma as *girija*), it follows that, as in other traditions, the source of the Rivers of Life is at the roots of the Tree of Life.

[23a] With Sarasvatī as a name of other-worldly significance, cf the "dogmatic" Boyne in Irish mythology, which takes its name from Bōann, wife of Nechtān (whom Rhys identifies with Neptune, and hence cognate with Varuṇa); this Boyne rises from "the well of the green of the fortress" (evidently a name of the Fountain of Life); it is "personified" as a queen, "slowly she moves, and yet her speed exceeds the pace of the swiftest steed," for "indeed, its waters traverse the whole world in seven years, which is more than the swiftest steed can do" (*see* Henderson, *Celtic Dragon Myth*, 1911, pp. xxxiv-xxxvi, and Joyce, *Old Celtic Romances*, 2nd ed., p. 187).

[24] For these meanings see my *New Approach to the Vedas*, Note 111 and cf. *Laṅkāvatāra Sūtra*, Ch. VI, text p. 228, "Appearance (*nimittam*) is characterised by local-position *saṁsthāna*)," etc.

Cf. St. Thomas, in *Opusculum de Pulchro et Bono*, citing Richard of S. Victor, *dicitur enim existens quasi ex alio sistens*.

For the expressions *caranti . . . nadyaḥ* and "Rivers of Life," cf. St. Thomas, *Sum. Theol.*, I, q. 18, a. 1, "Waters are called living that have a continuous current," and *Zohar* (Aḥare Moth) on Genesis II, 10, "that river . . . is called Life, because life issues thence to the world."

[25] "Eddying," inasmuch as the River of Life is ever at once outpouring and inflowing, never flowing straight away, as explained in J.U.B., I, 2. Cf. Jeremias, *Der Antichrist in Geschichte und Gegenwart*, 1930, p. 4, "Der Abendländer denkt linienhaft in die Ferne, darum mechanisch, areligiös, faustisch (this may be seen in the concept of an absolute evolution or progress). . . . Das Morgenland und die Bibel denken nicht linienhaft sondern zeitraumlich, spiralisch, kreislaufig. Das Weltgeschehen geht in Spiralen, die sich bis in die Vollendung fortsetzen." Inasmuch as the tide of life thus at the same time flows and ebbs, the Rivers of Life are sometimes spoken of as two, e.g., Vipāś and Sutudri in R.V., III, 33, cf. X, 30, 10, *āvarvṛtatīḥ* . . . *dvidharāḥ*, "two eddying floods."

[26] In metaphysical formulation, a "crossing of water" always implies a change of state and status, for example in the case of voyages to "otherworlds" (notably the Voyage of Bran, also in the Indian story of Maḥbūb, see my "Khwājā Khadir . . ." *Ars Islamica*, I, pp. 174-5, 1934), in the case of Charon and the Styx, and in the notions of "crossing over Jordan," and "one more river to cross." The First Crossing is a going forth towards a home "here"; the crossing back again, as of the River Vijarā ("ageless"), *Kauṣītaki* Up., I, 3, again effected by the intellect alone, and where now the traveller leaves behind him all the burden of his good or evil deeds (and all his memories), is the prodigal's return to the Father's home "there."

The formal aspects of the tradition as to "crossing water" have been admirably dealt with by Brown, *The Indian and Christian Miracles of Walking on the Water*, Chicago, 1928. J.B., II, 439, where the Rasā makes herself fordable for Indra's envoy, Saramā, may be added to the references discussed.

[27] This implies that the floor (*budhna*, "ground," R.V., X, 135, 6) is unwetted; that is, even whilst *en route*, the voyagers are safely supported by a platform resting, like every other "earth," or the lotus-leaf that symbolizes "earth," on the surface of the Sea. Cf. *preṅkha* in R.V., VII, 83, 3, and *naunagara* ("ark") in J.B., I, 125.

In R.V., VII, 18, the River crossed is the in-finite (*aditi*) Paruṣṇī ("turbulent"), or Yamunā (Griffiths remarks naïvely "it is not easy to see how the expedition reached so far"). Here again the waters grant an easy passage (*supārā*) to the Aryan party under Indra's guidance. The parallel with Exodus is here especially close, inasmuch as the opposing party is overwhelmed by the returning flood, after the passage of the Aryans.

That Exodus is a creation myth, rather than an historical event, is of course the Qabbalistic point of view. Note that Pharoah is described as "the great dragon (*tanim*, Babylonian *tiamat*) that lieth in the midst of his rivers, which has said, My river is mine own, and I have made it for myself" (Ezekiel, XXIX, 3); "spoiling the Egyptians" corresponds to the Devas taking possession of the kine and other treasures of the Asuras, e.g., R.V., II, 24, 6; and Moses to Indra, not only as leader of the chosen people, but in that he smites the Rock and finds Water for them in the wilderness.

According to the *Zohar* (Shelaḥ Lecha and Vaethhanan) "Moses was the Sun . . . Moses indeed made a new beginning in the world . . . there was that in Moses which was not in any other man, since his perfection radiated to many thousands and myriads."

[28] See the sections on *Carṣaṇi* and *Vāpa-maṅgala*.

[28a] As it may not be perfectly clear in what sense Essence (*ātman*) can be said to *separate* the worlds, it should be observed that B.U

IV, 4, 22, is careful to specify the aspect of the Essence which so functions as *vijñāna-maya*, "in the mode of discrimination," that is to say as the *mano-maya ātman*, or as the Com. glosses it, *jīvātman*. It is clear that the *ānanda-maya ātman*, or *paramātman*, could only be thought of as *uniting* the worlds.

The "Bridge" is often referred to simply as the "Path" (*pantha*) e.g., *Bṛhadaraṇyaka Up.* IV, 4, 8, "The strait ancient path outstretched . . . whereby the liberated Comprehensors of the Spiritual-power pass upward unto Paradise," and *Kaṭha Up.*, III, 14, "The sharpened edge of a razor, hard to be traversed, that the Seers call a difficult path," the latter passage corresponding also to *ib.* III, 2, "That bridge (*setuḥ*) for sacrificers, the imperishable and ultimate Spiritual-power, the Path (*pāram*) of them that would cross over to the place of No-fear, Nāciketas! it is that that we would master."

In R.V., X, 67, 4, where Bṛhaspati is said to drive forth "the hidden kine standing on the bridge of chaos" (*anṛtasya setau*), the bridge is evidently so called with respect to its "dark end," whence the procession of light is initiated; *anṛta* characterising the unordered, indiscriminate, potential, and dark world of the Asuras, *ṛta* the ordered and actual light world of the Devas. It is with respect to its "light end," and as being the pathway of angelic procession (*devayāna*) that the bridge is *amṛtasya*, "the bridge of aeviternity," as in M.U., II, 2, 5. It will be understood, of course, that here as always, the ultimate station of the Comprehensor (*vidvān*) is "in the middle place" (*madhye sthāne*, C.U., III, 2, 1), the "bridge," which is also the "axis of the universe," and "holds the worlds apart" having no longer any meaning or extension for him in whom the light and dark worlds are no longer divided.

Crossing, from the Wayfarer's point of view, is the passage from non-being to full being, hell to heaven, darkness to light, danger to safety; but because the place of safety considered only as the heaven of the manifested light is not the Comprehensor's final goal, Naciketas, in K.U., II, 11, is said to have "wholly renounced" that heavenly goal to which the bridge extends; for his goal is the Supreme Identity, *tad ekam* in R.V., I, 129, 2, wherein, as being without otherness, there is no distinction of darkness from light, death from aeviternal life, and therefore no yawning gap to be bridged over by a passage way.

28b Inasmuch as the "Bridge" appears in tradition oftener as the means of crossing back to the other world than as the means of coming forth, we have not thought it needful to give further references in the text. But another mention of the causeway linking *deva* and *asura* worlds should be noted in "Rāma's bridge," and though our conclusion is differently reached, we certainly agree with Charpentier (Bull. Sch. Or. Studies, VII, 682) that "There is not the slightest reason for suggesting that it (the *Rāmāyaṇa*) contains the story of the spread of Aryanism towards the South," and that "the apes are certainly not Dravidians." If Laṅkā is in the "South," it is as Nadir with respect to Zenith.

For the Cinvad Bridge see S.B.E., IV, 212, Note 3; and for other material, Scherman, *Materialen zur Geschichte der indischen Visionsliteratur*, 1892, p. 105, and Hull, *Cuchullin Saga*, 1898, pp. 72-76 and 291.

29 E. G. for China, see *Li Chi*, IV, 1, 1, 13 f., XXI, 2, 5-7, and XXI, 4-5 (S.B.E., Vols. XXVII, XXVIII), and also Granet, *Danses et Légendes de la Chine ancienne*, pp. 328-332. In the Chinese rite it is significant (1) that the ploughing is undertaken specifically to provide

the food required for offering in sacrifice, cf. VII, 2, 2, 7, cited below, (1) that there is a co-operation of male and female principles, the Empress and her ladies making the silk robes to be worn at the sacrifice, (3) that the opening of the ground, like the taking of virginity, is thought of as dangerous, and that it is the Emperor *qua* priest who takes this task upon himself, and (4) that a corresponding ritual with reversed significance was observed at the Autumn equinox.

[30] The Jambu tree prefigures and is virtually the Bodhi-tree; it is significant in this connection that here too there is an "awakening" —the Bodhisattva has been laid down by his father upon a bed (*sayana*) surrounded by an enclosing curtain, i.e., he is not "manifested," but he "rises up" (*uṭṭhāya*, i.e., proceeding from potentiality to act) to take his seat in *jhāna*. Such a rising up takes place at least four times in the course of the Bodhisattva's life, viz., at birth (*ṭhitako . . . paṭhaviyam patiṭṭhaya*, J., I, 53), then on the present occasion of the first *jhāna*, then at the going-forth (*abhinikkhamaṇa*, *ib.* I, 61, *sayana vuṭṭhaya*), finally when from rest in the *sāla*-grove he proceeds (*ib.* I, 70, *payasi* = *prayāti*) along a broadway to the Bodhi-tree. The use of root *sthā*, especially in connection with *śayana*, is technical, *cf.* Sayaṇa on .ṚV., V, 19, 1, *sthitam padārtha jātam*, and B.U., II, 3, 1, where what is *sthita* is also *mūrta*, and in Ṛ. V., I, 36, 13, *ūrddhva tiṣṭha*, I, 84, 3, *ā tiṣṭha*, III, 38, 4, *atiṣṭhat*, X, 53, 8, *uttiṣṭhata*, etc.

[31] The language of the verses in this Sutta is strongly reminiscent of Vedic texts; cf. e.g., *pamocanam* as "unyoking" with Ṛ.V., V, 46, 1, *vimucam*, III, 53, 20, *ā vimocanāt*; *mano yottam*, "intellect the yoke," with I, 51, 10, *manoyujaḥ*, II, 40, 3, *manasā yujyamānam*, V, 81, 1, *yuñjate mana*, and VII, 69, 2, *manasā yuktaḥ*; and note that the reward is "æviternity" (*amata-phala* = *amṛta-phala*).

[32] Ś.B., VII, 1, 2, 1, and 2, 2, 7; cf. P.B., 4, 10, 1, where the sacrifice is called a *maha vrata*, and the food consists of what ripens in a year (*saṁvatsaram annam pacyate*), this restores (*adhinot*) him.

"Food" is the *sine qua non* of existence (root *sthā*, Lat. *existare*, as distinguished from *esse*); *annam ad*, "to eat food," the Biblical "to find pasture" is technically "to exist," "live." Agni-Prajāpati, the principle and exemplar of all life, must be "fed" in order that the human sacrificer may likewise eat and live. It is from the same point of view that the Bodhisattva, before the Great Awakening, abandons his fast and takes food, for otherwise there could have been no public manifestation of his person; it will be understood of course that all the life as Bodhisattva Siddhārtha, antecedent to the Great Awakening, belongs to the operation *ab intra*, while the subsequent life as Buddha, "Awakened," and until the Parinirvāṇa, to the operation *ab extra*. The Son of Man comes "eating and drinking"; Agni is the "most greedy of eaters." Cf. B.U., 1, 2, 5, "He (Death) began to eat."

[33] Cf. Bagchi, P. C., *Pre-Aryan and pre-Dravidian in Indian*, 1929, pp. 10-15 (associates *liṅga* and *laṅgala* as having both the primitive meaning "virile member"); Langdon, *Semitic Mythology*, p. 99, citing Ebbeling, *Keilinschrifte aus Assur*, p. 319, "O my lord, the ploughshare hast thou caused to impregnate the earth"; Jeremias, *Old Testament in the Light of the Ancient East*, p. 59 ("In the Babylonian age . . . the planet Jupiter is designated 'Bull of the Sun,' and his place in the heavens 'Furrow of Heaven' . . . a plough is the attribute of Osiris . . . Nebuchadnezzar calls himself the husbandman (*ikkaru*) of Babylon"); and Sophocles, *Antigone*, 569.

Still more striking is the Sumerian text, "The astral Ploughman has yoked in the Plain (of Heaven) the seed-sowing Plough," cited by Frankfort in "Gods and myths in Sargonid seals," *Iraq*, I, 1934, p. 19, in connection with his Plate III, fig. h. This seal affords good support to the proposition that Vedic texts could be admirably illustrated not only from the later traditional art of India, such as has been made use of in our illustrations, but also from Sumerian and Babylonian seals; cf. in the same Journal, Plate I, fig. a, what may be said to represent at one and the same time the slaying of Tiamat, Herakles slaying the Hydra, and Indra slaying Vṛtra.

[34] See my *Yakṣas*, II, pp. 43-45, and references, *ib.* p. 43, Note 2.

[35] See Bloomfield in J.A.O.S., XVI, pp. 12-13.

[36] See the section Yama as Viśpati.

[37] Icelandic *land-náma*, whence the title of the present essay, with reference to the Icelandic "Book of the Taking of Land" by the ere-dwellers (*erbyggya*). The landfall of the Scandinavian immigrants in Iceland, like that of the first settlers in America, and that too of the Aryans in India (if we assume the existence of any such ethnic stock), all offer close analogies with the settlement of the worlds "in the beginning." This is a normal case of the correspondence of microcosm and macrocosm, cf. A.B., VIII, 2, *amuṣya lokasyayam loko' nurūpaḥ*, and A.A., III, 1, 2. In this sense every historical event is a "repeat of history" and a "recurrence."

From the Indonesians' point of view the same myth becomes their own pre-history, the legend of their own immediate origins. Every people makes of its own land a holy land in the likeness of the place of their origin, and names its sites after the names of places in the first homeland; that is in our case, as if desiring to establish a "kingdom of heaven on earth." As for the earthly altars, to adapt by changing a single word what has been aptly said by Mus ("Le Buddha paré . . ." B.É.F.E.O., 1928, pp. 252-253), "On dut les considérer commes de petits foyers, gardant pour ainsi dire un éclat des grandes forces actives concentrées aux sanctuaires privilégiés d'antan"; cf. Jeremias, *The Old Testament in the Light of the Ancient East*, p. 58.

[38] Corresponding to R.V., X, 14, 9, *asmā etam pitaro lokam akran*, both passages implying an establishment of worship *here* and that Yama is "not a God of the dead but of the living." Note that Vedic "here" and "this" refer to the Light-world generally, and not especially or exclusively to *our planet*.

Cf. R. V., VIII, 101, 14, "Three races digressed from the way, the others settled (*viviśre*) round the Light (*arkam*) . . . in the worlds": II, 1, 1, citing this text, adds, "those are settled down (*niviṣṭā*) around the Light, that is around Agni . . . even as being yonder Sun," where the application of *viś* to settlement in the Light-world is specific.

[39] From the Brāhmaṇa point of view at least, Agni and Prajāpati, the Year, are one and the same Demiurge, *anusaṁdhātṛ*.

The same idea is expressed in Christianity when Christ is spoken of as "mediate cause," as in St. Thomas, *Sum. Theol.*, I, q. 45, a. 6, *ad 2*, "the Son receives the power of creation from the Father . . . and of the Son it is said (John I. 3) 'Through Him all things were made.'"

[40] That the Devas are Asuras and Serpents sacrificially transformed or "turned about" (*paryāvṛtta*, etc.) is the theme of a separate article, entitled "Angel and Titan, an essay in Vedic ontology," to appear in the J.A.O.S. this year.

That the Serpents "change their skins" is represented throughout the Indian tradition in the power attributed to "Nāgas" of assuming a serpentine or "human" form at will. "Creeping farther" recalls *vi ca sarpata atas* in R.V., X, 14, 9, which according to our understanding is said with reference to angelic procession, and the lengthening of days and prolongation of one's line, as in X, 18, 3 and 6: contrast *avasarpaṇa* in S.B., 1, 8, 1, 7, cf. Note.

[41] The *plakṣa prāsravaṇa* is also referred to as a "pool," *hrada*. In the various accounts of the rejuvenation of Cyavāna (R.V., I, 116, 10, P.B., XXV, 6, 10, Ś.B., IV, 1, 5, J.B., III, 120 and 125, etc.) the pool in which his youth is renewed by the Aśvins is referred to either as such (*hrada*), or as Waters (*apaḥ*), or as the "infancy" (*śaiśava*) of the Sarasvatī, and must be regarded as the same as the source (*prāsravaṇa*) of the Sarasvatī referred to in P.B., XXV, 10, 16, and *utsa akṣita* and *sindhūnām upodaya* of R.V., VIII, 17, 16 and 41, 8. It would also seem to follow that Cyavāna, "in decline," should be regarded as a designation of Prajāpati, when "stupefied by age," *jīryya mūra* (P.B., XXV, 17, 3). Cf. P. B., XXV, 15, 4, *hitvā jīrṇān tacam* (of which there is a reminiscence in *Bhagavad Gītā*, II, 22, *vāsāṅsi jīrṇāni yathā vihāya*).

Agni, commonly (as in Ś.B.) and rightly identified with Prajāpati, is similarly subject to inveteration at the end of a world age, cf. R.V. II, 4, 5, "Being aged, He forthwith became a youth again" (*jujurvān yo muhur ā yuvā bhūt*), and A.A., II, 1, 7, where the powers (*vibhūtayah*, sc. *devas*) of the *Puruṣa* are said to endure "so long as the world of Fire and Earth does not grow old" (*na jīryate*). An ageing of the worlds, and of the manifested principle of life by which they are animated, is necessarily involved in the traditional doctrine of aeonic succession. Cyavāna, then, may be taken to be an epithet of Agni-Prajāpati at the end of an aeon: cf. R.V., V, 74, 5, "Ye (Aśvins) took off from the inveterated Cyavāna (*jujuruṣo cyavānāt*) his skin as it were a robe (*vavrim atkam na muñcathaḥ*), then when ye made him young again (*yuvā . . . punaḥ*) he stirred the Bride's desire" (*ā kāmaṁ ṛṇve vadhvaḥ*). We may say, made him once more that potent *pati* for whom "the desirous woman goes a seeking in the flood," J.U.B., I, 56: and all this corresponds to R.V., VII, 101, 3, "Now is He impotent, and now becomes progenitive, He shapes his likeness as He will." At the dawn of a new age, therefore, the former powers are said to "fall away" (*cyu*), as in R.V., X, 124, 4, *agniḥ somo varuṇas te cyavante*; or alternatively, as having fallen away (*cyavāna*), to change their skins, proceeding in renewed youth. Here then, and just as in other traditions, we recognize the concept of a Dying God and ever recurrent Resurrection; One Principle, outwardly subject to an aeviternal inveteration (*jarā*) but having at the same time in Itself an unageing life (*āyuḥ ajaram*, X, 51, 7) and altogether independent of time (*ajuryam*, X, 88, 13); mortal and immortal, manifested and unshown, moving and unmoved. Sol Invictus: "All else that moves comes to rest, only the Waters ever flow, the Sun for ever rises . . . Who with thy Light dispellest Darkness, and with thy Radiance settest all in motion" (R.V., X, 37, 2 and 4). "He indeed never really rises nor sets, but only inverts himself" (*Aitareya Brāhmaṇa*, III, 44).

The *hrada* or *śaiśava* of the Sarasvatī, the Fountain of Life cited above, is also the same as the *āvatta* of the Nerañjanā, the abode of Kāla Nāgarāja, to which the Buddha's *pātra* floats upstream (*paṭisotam*), a distance of "eighty 'hands' by measure with the speed of a swift horse"; the same as Kāliya's whirlpool of the Yamunā in the Kṛṣṇa *līlā*; and the same as the whirlpool in the Story of Prince Maḥbūb (Chilli, *Folk Tales of Hindustan*).

41a This is the normal, rather than in any sense a peculiar point of view; cf. for example, "The Christian Sacrifice (the Mass) . . . is an act of the divine and eternal order the reality and significance of which can only be seen when it is viewed in the context of eternity. It is not confined to, nor limited by, the conditions of time and space, yet since it concerns man who is a creature of time and space as well as an heir of eternity it is immersed in the moments of our time" (Bede Frost, *The Meaning of Mass*, Oxford, 1934, p. 63).

42 *Avabhraṁśana* must be understood here in the inverted, favourable, upstream sense, not as in A.V., XIX, 39, 8.

For Alexander's analogous search for the Fountain of Life in the Land of Darkness, and other Persian analogies see the sources cited in my "Khwājā Khadir and the Fountain of Life . . ." in *Ars Islamica*, Part 2, 1934; and for a Chinese parallel, the lost Vale of the Immortals and the Fountain at the River's Source, Hefter and Hall, "The Chinese Idyll," *China Journal of Sciences and Arts*, XXV, May, 1934, pp. 220 ff. If the journey upstream be a "myth," how can the journey downstream, which is presupposed, have been a "fact"?

43 In the same way X, 56, has primarily to do with the procession of Agni and the Patriarchs, with a voyaging in the ship of life within the worlds, "whether by these or farther shores" (*avariṣu, pareṣu*).

44 "Man-regarding," *nṛcakṣa*, R.V., X, 14, 11, elsewhere in R.V. said of Savitṛ, Agni, Soma, *viśvedevāḥ*, *pitaraḥ*, etc., always in a favourable sense, cf. Sāyaṇa on X, 158, 8, *nṛcakṣa* = "harmful to the foes of men."

45 Cf. the popular (traditional) expressions "blindworm" and "deaf adder."

46 *Visarpaṇa* and *atisarpaṇa* implied in the cited passages are the opposite of *avasarpaṇa* in Ś.B., I, 8, 1, 7 = *avaprabhraṁśana* in A.V., XIX, 39, 8. Cf. the case of Apālā, on whom Indra bestowed a "solar skin" (*sūrya-tvacam*) in place of the scaly skins that are removed when she is passed through holes in the celestial chariot, which represent the gateway of procession (R.V., VIII, 91, with Sāyaṇa's gloss). Even more significant, in view of the known relationship between Ahi Budhnya, the Chthonic Serpent (cf. R.V., VII, 34, 16, *ahim abjām budhne nadīnām rajaḥsu ṣidan*) and Agni Gārhapatya, the Household Fire (cf. A.B., III, 36) is the finding of Agni "on a lotus leaf where he had crept up out of the Waters" (*adbhya upôdāsṛptam puṣkaraparṇe*, Ś.B., VII, 3, 2, 14); the use of *sṛp* here admirably illustrates the unfailing precision of the traditional texts.

Observe also that in Buddhism, the list of those disqualified from admission to the Saṁgha, the "Ariyan" community, includes eunuchs (in R.V., the defeated and excluded powers of darkness are typically *vadhri*, *mūra*, and *stari*) and serpents; thus very evidently preserving the pattern of the original Vedic distinction of *ārya* from *anārya*.

It may be noted further in this connection that Buddhism similarly carries over from the *Ṛg Veda* the notion of *arhatta*, "fitness," "qualification," or "proficiency." The designation *arhat* is applied to Agni in II, 3, 1 and 3 and X, 2, 2, to Indrâgnī in V, 86, 5, to Indra in X, 99, 7, to Rudra in II, 33, 10, to the Maruts in V, 52, 5, and to the First Sacrificers in V, 7, 2, while in X, 63, 4, it is "by *arhaṇa*" that the Ādityas are said to "obtain their aeviternity (*amṛtatvam ānaśuḥ*), the trace of their earlier state remaining in the designation *ahi-māyā*, "possessing the magic of the serpent"; *māyā* here, as generally, pertaining to the *asuratva* that remains in the *devas*, and by which they operate.

The parallel in Matthew, X, 16, *estote ergo prudentes sicut serpentes, et simplices sicut columbae* represents more than a simple figure of speech.

Apropos of our three illustrations, derived from Jaina sources, it may be added that Jainism, no less than Buddhism, preserves the Vedic "*arhat*," see the description of Fig. 2. And if the designation "Maker of a ford ' (*tīrthaṁkara*) does not occur as such in the *Ṛg Veda*, the notion involved in any case corresponds to what is an essential function of the *viśpati* who conducts the kindreds across the flowing Waters to the promised lands; cf. also X, 30, 14, where the prayer is addressed to the Aśvins, "Make ye a ford" (*kṛtam tīrtham*), and various other passages in which the word *tīrtha* appears. It may be noted, too, that just as Mahāvīra is conceived by one mother and nurtured by another, so in Buddhism, Siddhârtha is born of one who dies immediately, and is nurtured by her sister, these two bearing the significant names Māyā and Pajāpatī, which represent in fact the names of the Madonna respectively in eternity, and in aeviternity or time, at "night" and by "day." This dual birth immediately reflects that of the "two-mothered *dvimātā*) Agni of the *Ṛg Veda*, as for example in III, 55, 4, where "One mother holds the Calf (Skr. *vatsa* = bambino, just as speaking in the vernacular we sometimes call a child a "kid"), the other rests" (*kṣeti* = remains *ab intra*, as in III, 55, 7, and X, 51, 5); while in V, 2, 2, we see that of these two mothers, it is the Queen-mother (*mahiṣī*, corresponding to the Buddhist Māyā) that begets the Prince (*kumār* = Agni), and the "handmaid" (*peṣī*, corresponding to Pajāpatī in the Buddhist legend) that is now holding him. An almost literal parallel to the events of Mahâvīra's nativity occurs in R.V., I, 113, 1, where "Night, as having conceived for Savitr's quickening (*prasūtā savituḥ savāya*) yields the womb to Dawn" (*yonim āraik*), cf. I, 124, 8, "Sister to mightier sister yields the womb."

Other correspondences between the Buddha and Agni are demonstrated in my *Elements of Buddhist Iconography*, Cambridge, 1935. To materials assembled there it may be added that the *Buddhacarita*, I, 16 and II, 19-20, referring to the death of Māyā-devi after the birth of Siddhârtha, describes her as "abandoning, as was befitting, her subtle form (*sūkṣmaṁ prakṛtim*) and manifesting her 'double' (*svamūrtiḥ*), of the disposition with herself (*sama-prabhāvā*)." In this less rationalised form, the story corresponds to the Vedic myth of Vivasvat (the Sun) and his wife Saraṇyū, whose son is Yama, and Saraṇyū's "double" (savarṇā) whose son is Manu (Yama and Manu can both be identified with or assimilated to Agni). There can be no question that the legends of Mahâvīra and Buddha are adaptations, or rather, partial rationalisations, of the Vedic legend of Agni, in which the historical element is absent. It is accordingly that we can say that like the stories, the traditional illustrations of the nativities of Mahâvīra and Buddha are virtually illustrations of the nativity of Agni and representations of the Creation "in the beginning" as described in the *Ṛg Veda*.

It may be added, recalling at the same time that the name Viṣṇu is of frequent occurrence in the *Ṛg Veda* as a designation of the Sun, that the legend of Kṛṣṇa's nativity once more repeats the essentials of the story as summarised above. Born of Vasudeva and Devakī in the realm of an Asura, Kṛṣṇa is conveyed to Gokula (the Braja-maṇḍala is not this Gokula, but called after it), where he is fostered by Yaśodā, who like Triśalā does not know that the child was not begotten in her own womb: the translation from interior to exterior operation is clearly marked by the miraculous crossing of the river Jamunā, which though in flood, becomes fordable at the touch of Kṛṣṇa's foot, the story thus repeating with only slight variation the Vedic legend of the First Crossing of the River of Life, "leaving behind the unfriendly powers" (R.V., X, 53, 8), and it will not be overlooked that the real mother "remains" (Vedic *kṣeti*) within. The parallels could be developed at great length; most of Kṛṣṇa's heroic feats, for example, are the same as Indra's or Agni's.

[47] The "estimative understanding" in scholastic definition; appetitive, pragmatic, experimental, scientific knowledge.

[48] It has often been remarked that a doctrine of Hell is unknown to the Ṛg Veda. In fact, however, the Ṛg Vedic Hell is precisely that ante-natal tomb from which the life-desirous principles are thought of as escaping, or into which those who have fallen into metaphysical sin or are enemies of the Aryan Kindreds may be thrust back again. On the other hand, the intermediate state of latency (privation) is a *future* one only from the standpoint of those already manifested in any æon who, being progenitively inclined (*prajā-kāmya*) and occupied with works, have not yet as Comprehensors (*vidvān*) risen above the "storm of the world-flow." Wherever the evolution and involution of worlds is thought of as an eternal cycle, "Hell" or restraint is necessarily a past as well as a future state contrasted with that of the worlds themselves, in which the satisfaction of desires is freely pursued.

At the same time, it is only from the mundane (*laukika*) point of view that the state of privation can and must be thought of as one of defect; the privation is more strictly speaking an absence of any limiting condition, a liberty (*adititva*) that is not in any wise (*nêti, nêti*), but potentially in all wise (*viśvatas*, etc.), for "What is silent (*tuṣīm* = *maunam*) is unexpounded (*aniruktam*), and what is unexpounded is everything (*sarvvam*)," Ś.B., VII, 2, 2, 14, cf. Eckhart, "This impotence of the essence is its chief potentiality."

[49] This essential name of Agni, as he who *akhyat devānām janimā*, R.V., IV, 2, 18, and *viśvā veda janimā*, VI, 15, 13, is here especially appropriate.

[50] The last reference is to the "tortures of hell," in the senses aforesaid, cf. for example R.V., IV, 19, 9, where the "Maiden's Son" (Agni) is spoken of as "blind and devoured by ants." Of Agni as eighth Āditya, Martāṇḍa, Agni Vaiśvānara, Agni-Prajāpati, it may assuredly be said that "he descends into Hell and rises again from the dead," *punaḥ punaḥ jāyamāna*.

[51] An ambiguity that recurs in connection with every symbolic representation of the cosmic cycle. The Tree of Life, for example,

is one to be fostered or felled according to our point of view, see texts cited in my *Elements of Buddhist Symbolism*, pp. 11-12. And without multiplying Indian instances, it may be pointed out that just as in the case of the funeral hymns of the *Ṛg Veda*, so in that of the funeral texts of the solar cult in ancient Egypt, it is very evident that these are worded originally with respect to the divine procession, and only secondarily adapted inversely. This becomes especially obvious when we find the Pharaoh (Teti) called upon to come to the rescue of "the Sun (Atum) in darkness"—the Vedic *gūḷham sūryam*, V, 40, 6, etc.—"to kindle for him the light and to protect him," see J. H. Breasted, *The Dawn of Conscience*, 1934, p. 87.

52 Needless to say that from the *jñāna kāṇḍa* point of view, so familiar in Buddhist formulation, the "crossing over" to be accomplished by the Comprehensor, or for him by the Angel of his devotion and of whom he partakes (*bhakti* = "participation"), is not as it was in the beginning hitherward, but hence; for as Eckhart expresses it, "the last end is the same as the first beginning."

53 Monotony of implication (*ekavṛttatva*) or sameness (*samatā*), not without variety of explication (*vivṛttatva*), but comparable to that of water flowing from a perennial source, or that of the recurrent seasons. If we are never wearied by the recital of what is always the same story, this is in the same sense that we are never wearied of the daily rising and setting of the sun: we often *demand* "novelty" when our attention is distracted, but whenever we regard the realities of life, we recognize that what we really *need* is not a perpetually "novel" but a constantly "original" (*ex fonte*) experience.